S C O

Ghost Stories

Prepare to be frightened by these terrifying tales
from around Scotland

By

Richard Holland

BRADWELL
BOOKS

Published by Bradwell Books
9 Orgreave Close Sheffield S13 9NP
Email: books@bradwellbooks.co.uk

© Richard Holland 2013

1st Edition

ISBN: 9781902674728

Print: Gomer Press, Llandysul, Ceredigion SA44 4JL

Design by: jenksdesign@yahoo.co.uk

Photograph Credits: Shutterstock and Alan Daulby

CONTENTS

INTRODUCTION

Scotland is a proud nation whose roots begin with a prehistoric race which almost uniquely in Europe was never conquered by the Romans: the Picts. By the early historical period this far northern land had also become peopled with Celts (both Gaels and Britons), Norsemen in parts of the far north and west and Angles in parts of the south and east. Together they formed a culturally and politically distinct nation recognised as a power in Europe and which remained a particular thorn in the side of England for centuries. Edinburgh became a cultural centre of global importance by the dawn of the 19th century and Glasgow one of the powerhouses of the Industrial Revolution.

Scotland's landscape reflects its distinctive character. The Highlands are the only places remaining in Britain where true wilderness can be found. Remnants of the ancient pine forests that formerly covered much of northern Europe linger here and the country harbours fauna and flora found nowhere else in the UK – maybe even a lake monster or two! From Shetland and the Outer Hebrides, through the high peaks and deep glens of the Grampians and the Cairngorms, into the pastoral Lowlands, Scotland is steeped in mystery and legend.

The ghosts of Scotland are as wild and as fascinating as the land they haunt. Here can be encountered apparitions of Highlanders and Redcoats, pipers and harpers, fierce knights and wicked magicians, disembodied heads and hands and monstrous beings that are barely human. In addition there are the ghosts of celebrities like Walter Scott and Bonnie Prince Charlie and those of anonymous folk: monks, nuns, sailors, maid servants and factory workers. There are also numerous phantom ladies, invariably named after the colour of the gowns they are seen wearing: green or grey, pink or white.

The tales of tragedy or romance behind the ghosts are often as interesting as the hauntings themselves and the places they haunt are well worth a visit for their history and beauty, as well as for their legends. Scotland is blessed with a wealth of imposing castles and grand houses and many of them are haunted. So too are a number of its moors and mountains. There are even a couple of haunted beaches.

The scope of this book can only hint at the full extent of Scotland's haunted heritage, so I hope it will inspire you to explore this absorbing subject further.

Richard Holland

*The Royal Mile, Edinburgh, is a stretch of the most haunted real
estate in the world.*
Brendan Howard/Shutterstock

EDINBURGH

Scotland's capital is almost unrivalled for the number of haunted sites it can offer. Only London can dispute its title of the most haunted city in Britain. But no city has made more of its haunted heritage than Edinburgh. There are at least two tourist attractions whose main appeal is the ghosts allegedly haunting them.

The best known of these is 'Real Mary King's Close'. Mary King's Close is a rare survivor of medieval Edinburgh, a narrow street which was shut off during an outbreak of plague in the 17th century and afterwards buried and therefore preserved beneath subsequent building. Shut off from the modern world and a place where many people died in squalor, it is undeniably creepy. Other than the possible spirit of a small girl (for whom tourists still leave gifts), the Close's haunted reputation today rests largely on the feelings of unease experienced by hundreds of visitors every year and by the 'orbs' and odd 'mists' and other light anomalies picked up on cameras.

Nonetheless, paranormal activity was first reported here centuries ago. Mr Thomas Coltheart was one of the few people to risk moving back into Mary King's Close after the plague had subsided and he found the now-enclosed area had become badly haunted. He claimed he and his family became the victims of considerable disturbance, unsettling poltergeist activity and the startling appearance of disembodied hands and heads. In a weird twist of fate, Coltheart himself became a ghost: his form was seen by a number of witnesses after his death.

The Niddry Street Vaults is another very spooky place, historically interesting but very much marketed for its haunted reputation. The Vaults consists of an entirely enclosed series of chambers within a city bridge. They were rediscovered in the 1980s. Scores of people died in a fire in the Vaults in 1824 and this may have inspired the phenomena which became known 'the South Bridge Poltergeist' in the following decades.

After the Vaults reopened as a tourist attraction in 1996, more spooky activity has been reported. The various presences and apparitions are of uncertain identity and include 'the Watcher', a solitary, silent apparition of a man in a long cloak. An invisible force, which pushes and shoves visitors, is said to exist in one chamber and in another a gang of burly builders fled in a panic after being pelted with stones and seeing their equipment being moved about. Dr Richard Wiseman of the University of Hertfordshire ran an investigation here, monitoring the experiences of volunteers spending hours on their own in separate vaults. One heard breathing and another saw a figure wearing an apron. Variations in magnetic fields and air movements were recorded from the 'haunted' chambers.

Edinburgh is one of Europe's most exciting and historical cities. Its haunted heritage too is arguably second to none.
vichie81/Shutterstock

The most 'touristy' part of Edinburgh is the 'Royal Mile', a series of streets that run from the Castle eastwards to Holyrood Palace for a distance of about a Scots mile, a defunct unit of measure which was about three-hundred yards longer than an English mile. A walk down the Royal Mile passes many of Edinburgh's haunted sites.

An extraordinary number of ghosts are claimed for Edinburgh Castle. A phantom drummer boy is believed to patrol the battlements, thumping out a loud tattoo as a warning of coming calamity. The apparition of a former prisoner also haunts the battlements, where he died centuries ago in a reckless bid for freedom. The ghost of Janet Douglas, Lady of Glamis, who was executed here in the 16th century for conspiracy to murder King James V, wanders in various parts of the castle. A ghostly dog has been seen in the area of the old pets' cemetery and spectral cats have been seen in one of the houses within the castle walls. The sound of a galloping horse has been heard late at night thundering over the bridge and past the guardroom.

Eerie laughter and dismal groans have been heard in the Vaults below the castle and the brutal sounds of a murder committed way back in 1689 have been heard again in more recent times in the Governor's House. Another paranormal phenomenon to watch out for is the behaviour of an old soldier's tunic kept on display in a glass case in the restaurant. Staff have reported seeing the tunic move by itself as if someone is wearing it.

Beyond the castle walls, Castle Hill is said to be the haunt of the infamous Deacon William Brodie. Brodie was a seemingly respectable businessman and councillor who led a double life as a burglar, using his ill-gotten gains to fund two mistresses and five illegitimate children. He was the inspiration for Robert Louis Stevenson's Dr Jekyll and Mr Hyde. The ghost is described as a shadowy figure carrying a lantern through the narrow streets (known as wynds) which radiate from Castle Hill: its identification as Brodie may just be wishful thinking.

Edinburgh Castle is not only an impressive landmark, it is one of the most haunted places in Scotland.
Heartland/Shutterstock

Further down the Royal Mile, Castle Hill becomes the High Street, dominated by St Giles Cathedral. Some years ago a Mrs Porter had an eerie experience in the cathedral. She was in the transept when she suddenly felt 'a sharp blow on her back'. Shocked, she turned round to tell off whoever had done it, only to find there was no one there. Puzzled and a little frightened, she walked on but moments later she felt a second blow in her back. The same thing happened a third time. Again, no one was visible to account for the assault. Now thoroughly scared, Mrs Porter hurried over to an official of the cathedral, who told her that she was not alone in experiencing the weird phenomenon. Gravely, he added that it was considered an omen and that she should prepare herself for some bad news. Unfortunately, he was proved correct, for later that day Mrs Porter received the tragic news that her son had met with a fatal accident. He died at noon, the precise time Mrs Porter had had her strange experience in the cathedral.

Nearby is the Mercat (or Market) Cross. This originally stood at the spot indicated by the design laid out on the pavement but what remains of it has since been incorporated into the impressive 19th century monument. On September 9, 1513, the Mercat Cross became possessed of weird spirits. It was the night before the Battle of Flodden which took place in Northumbria between a Scots army and English defenders. As the cannon were being wheeled past on their way south to Northumberland, 'ghostly heralds' appeared on the cross and gloomily intoned the names of all those sons of Edinburgh who were to die in the battle. They were pointedly ignored, except by one man, Sir Richard Lawson, who on hearing his name, called out to the spirits: 'I appeal from your justice, judgment and sentence, and betake me all hail to the mercy of God.' He was the only man named by the spirits to return alive from the devastating defeat at Flodden Field.

*St Giles Cathedral in Edinburgh's High Street is haunted by
an invisible but ominous ghost.*
PlusONE/Shutterstock

The Mitre Bar, further down the High Street, gets its name from
having been the former home of a controversial cleric,
Archbishop Spottiswode. Spottiswode fled Edinburgh when he
learned he was about to lose his position thanks to his hell-
raising life. Legend has it that in a secret, walled-up alcove in
his house he hid his robes and even the imposing chair he'd used
in the Cathedral. He died on the way to London and any hidden
valuables have never been found. Spottiswode's ghost has

regularly been seen in the Mitre over the years and he is blamed for occasional inexplicable incidents such as the moving around of bottles and glasses, weird electrical disturbances and the occasional physical contact – one visitor to the pub claimed he was shoved in the back by something invisible (a phenomenon also recorded from the Cathedral).

The High Street becomes Canongate as one heads further east and here can be found an old house which has been named 'Bible Land' after the sculpture of an open Bible above its main entrance. Centuries ago a woman was murdered on the top floor of Bible Land and her ghost began to haunt the scene of the crime. She appeared as she was at the time of her cruel death, in a tartan dress with an apron over it and a white linen cap known as a 'mutch' upon her head. She became such a familiar sight in the building that the residents treated her almost as a friend.

The Tolbooth Inn stands next door to the Tolbooth, with its clock tower. The ghosts of two men in 'old-fashioned military costumes' have been seen in this historic pub and staff have also glimpsed a number of less distinct figures. Mild poltergeist activity – for example, the moving of objects and the occasional smashing of a glass – has been witnessed in the dining area at the rear of the tavern. One customer watched fascinated as an invisible hand pulled books off a shelf and dropped them on to the floor.

The weird emblem above the door of 'Bible Land', an ancient haunted house on Canongate.
© Alan Daulby

Near the end of the Royal Mile is 16th century Queensbury House, which has now been incorporated into the Scottish Parliament complex. Alas, the high security fences built around it have spoilt its appearance more than a little. A gruesome legend is attached to Queensbury House. In the early 18th century, it is said, the son of the then owner of the house, James, Second Duke of Queensberry, had a grim secret – his own son was a raving lunatic, and he kept him locked up and away from prying eyes. The youth was more like a beast than a man and had a ravenous hunger.

One fateful day, he escaped from his cell in the bowels of the house and, drawn by the smell of roasting meat, found his way to the kitchen. The kitchen was deserted except for a small boy who was employed to turn the meat on the spit over the fire. When the Duke and his men returned to the house, they found the kitchen in a mess, half the meat gnawed off the spit, and the maniac sitting on a stool by the fire, placidly devouring what remained of the kitchen boy! Ever since this horrific cannibal feast, the site of the old kitchens has been haunted by the unfortunate boy and also by the smell of roasting meat. Staff have complained of strange goings-on in the area (now occupied by an administration office) as recently as 2009.

The Royal Mile comes to an end at another of Edinburgh's star attractions and another with a ghostly reputation: Holyrood Palace. For many years Holyrood Palace was possessed of an indelible bloodstain which commemorated the assassination of the lover of Mary, Queen of Scots, a man named Rizzio. Under Rizzio's dead body, the blood pooled from a gaping sword wound onto the floorboards and for a long time the stain could not be got rid of, never mind how often it was scrubbed by overworked servants.

A number of apparitions have also been seen at Holyrood. The Grey Lady is the most commonly encountered, drifting quietly here and there and keeping her secret, for no one knows who she is or why she should haunt the Palace. A man dressed in the style of the 16th century with a ruff round his neck has also been seen. It's possible this is the ghost of Lord Darnley, Mary, Queen of Scots' husband. Phantom footfalls have regularly been heard pacing empty corridors. Lady Tweedale, who lived in the Palace in the 1890s, related several psychic experiences. These included seeing a man dressed in the style of the Restoration walking through a door and watching as a heavy iron bedstead moved itself across a bedroom floor.

If all these individual haunted sites were not enough, the entire length of the Royal Mile itself is haunted. The ghost of General Tam Dalyell, a Scottish Royalist defeated during the Civil War, charges down street after street riding a spectral horse. A phantom black coach pulled by black horses has also been known to thunder along the Royal Mile. Legend has it the entrance to a tunnel was uncovered at Edinburgh Castle centuries ago and a piper was sent down with a lantern to trace its course. He played his bagpipes with all his might so that those above ground could follow the direction he took. Suddenly the sound ceased and he was never seen again. Now, if you listen very carefully, you might hear the mournful skirl of his pipes somewhere deep below your feet on the Royal Mile.

A number of apparitions, most commonly that of a lady in grey, have been
reported from Holyrood Palace.
TanArt/Shutterstock

Just off the Royal Mile is another area popular with tourists, the Grassmarket. Centuries ago the Grassmarket was haunted by Major Weir, a self-confessed devil-worshipper who was executed along with his sister in the 17th century. Major Weir's satanic ghost gallops through the Grassmarket on a headless horse wreathed in flames. The apparition of Jean Weir, who was burned to death alongside her brother after cheerfully admitting to being a witch, has also been seen here, with a face horribly blackened and disfigured from the flames. Their ghosts have also been encountered near their former home in West Bow.

Finally, we must consider Greyfriars Kirkyard, complete with its statue of 'Greyfriars Bobby', the little terrier whose refusal to quit the burial place of his master made him famous. Nowadays, thanks in part to a number of regular ghost tours, Greyfriars is just as well known for its spooks. Many people attending these tours have reported unpleasant experiences in the southern part of the graveyard, where can be found the 'Covenanters' Prison'. Here, in the 17th century, scores of people who had sought religious independence were locked up on suspicion of treason. So harsh was their treatment that many of these men, women and children died. Numerous visitors claim to have experienced overwhelming feelings of dread and nausea in and around the Covenanters' Prison and a few have even passed out.

Others claim to have been pushed, slapped or pinched by something invisible and malevolent, particularly near the monument to Sir George MacKenzie Rosehaugh, the man responsible for the Covenanters' fate. 'Bloody' MacKenzie's mausoleum has been long been considered haunted. In recent years a weird glowing figure has also been reported from the Kirkyard.

*A massacre in Greyfriars Churchyard in the 17th century has generated
a plethora of psychic phenomena in the vicinity of the so-called
'Covenanters' Prison'.* © *Alan Daulby*

GLASGOW

Glasgow's largest city also has its fair share of ghosts. The apparition of two men in 18th century costume has been seen in the vicinity of George Street. They are a cheerful pair, strolling along and chatting amicably – although silently – to each other. They were seen by a shift-worker returning home in the small hours of the morning. They ambled along beside him for a while, exchanging their silent gossip, and then, in the wink of an eye, vanished.

The late ghost-hunter Andrew Green recorded a case of haunting at one of the road bridges over the River Clyde in Central Glasgow. A friend of Green's was walking over the Dalmarnock Road Bridge when he saw: 'A normal-looking young man, standing on the bridge looking down towards the Clyde. Thinking it may be a suicide attempt, I suddenly found myself shouting, "No, don't", but when only three yards from him, the man jumped … As I looked over the bridge in horror, I was utterly amazed to see the figure vanish into thin air.' The witness was so shocked by the vision that it made him feel physically sick. He was able to recall the ghost's appearance in detail, as 'a youngish man of about thirty wearing a navy-blue three-quarter length coat, and coal black trousers. He has his hair in a crew-cut style.'

In his book *Ghosts of Today*, Andrew Green also relates an odd experience had by a customer in a now defunct clothes shop in Brunswick Street. She was browsing the outfits on display when she noticed a middle-aged man sitting cross-legged on a chair in the middle of the store, reading a paper which he held in one hand. He only caught her attention because the shop was crowded and he was sitting in an inconvenient place utterly unconcerned by the bustle round him. The cut of his suit was rather old-fashioned and in a material heavier than one would expect on a warm summer's day. The customer was just noticing these apparently inconsequential details when suddenly both man and chair disappeared. One moment he was there, the next he was gone. No explanation has come forward to this mundane but puzzling apparition.

One of the city's most haunted locations is its Western Infirmary. Many hospitals all over the UK have haunted reputations, due perhaps to the dramas of life and death which take place in them. Numerous are the tales of night staff hearing disembodied footsteps approaching the beds of dying patients or seeing apparitions apparently watching over them.

The ghost of the Western Infirmary is said to be of a renowned surgeon. The story, as told by Peter Underwood in his *Gazetteer of Scottish and Irish Ghosts*, is that brain surgeon Sir William McEwan, near the end of his life, turned away an artist who was suffering from blinding headaches. The headaches were not only painful and debilitating, they were seriously interfering with his work and he was desperate. Nevertheless, after repeated requests, Sir William declined to carry out an operation, possibly because he felt his own skill was fading. After a heated consultation, the artist, in the midst of one of his attacks, left the office of the unresponsive Sir William and, in his anguish and agony, tripped on the staircase and fell to his death. The ghostly white-coated figure which has been encountered pacing a corridor leading to an operating theatre after dark is now thought to be Sir William's remorseful spirit.

Glasgow's Theatre Royal is haunted by a less exalted figure: a humble cleaner. Nicknamed 'Nora' by staff, this unassuming apparition goes about its mundane tasks just as Nora did in life. Another female phantom patrols one of the city's more unusual haunted sites: one of the Underground stations. The 'Grey Lady' is the name given to the ghost of the station in Shields Road, Kingston. The story given to explain her presence is that she fell onto the tracks in the 1920s and was killed. Mysterious footsteps have also been heard here and maintenance crews have reported seeing 'weird lights' around the station.

The city of Glasgow is the location of a number of extraordinary ghost stories.
Claudio Divizia/Shutterstock

The creepiest location in Glasgow is its Necropolis, an extensive cemetery distinguished by ornate gothic tombs of the 19th century. Actually there are two cemeteries. The Southern Necropolis is in the Gorbals. Several odd stories are told about the Southern Necropolis. According to organisers of ghost walks here, a statue on the memorial to the innocuously named Mrs Smith has a habit of turning its head to stare at passers-by! Even stranger is the incident which took place in the 1960s, when gangs of Gorbals kids invaded the cemetery in search of a vampire. This was no ordinary vampire (if there is such a thing): this one had metal fangs. The youngsters were so convinced of the existence of this monster and its predations on local schoolchildren that they formed a posse, armed themselves with stakes, and set off to dispatch it. The police had to be called to calm the situation. It is thought a pulp horror comic may have inspired the belief in the Vampire with Iron Teeth.

A number of other strange tales about Glasgow have been related by the late ghost-hunter Elliott O'Donnell. One of the most bizarre concerns a haunted bath. O'Donnell is notorious for his very many weird and wonderful ghost stories which are rarely supported by named witnesses or even specific locations, thereby stretching credulity to its limit. In this case, however, he provides both: the witness is given as a Captain W. de S. Smythe and the location as a house in Blythswood Square. He does not identify the house specifically, but this would be a reasonable precaution against litigation from an aggrieved landlord who might find it hard to let a house with a haunted reputation. According to O'Donnell, Capt Smythe was delighted with everything in the house when he moved in except the bathroom. This he found 'excessively grim'. Even after a major overhaul and redecoration there was something about this room which he found vaguely unnerving.

Nothing untoward happened here until the Smythes had been in residence for a number of weeks. When Capt Smythe was preparing to take a bath, he heard some odd noises coming from a grate. He chose to ignore them. After a few aborted attempts to get in the bath – the water always seemed too hot – he slipped on the wet floor and fell with an undignified bump. Before he had the chance to clamber up again, the candles he had lit suddenly went out and he found himself 'engulfed in the most funereal darkness'. O'Donnell takes up the tale:

'The moment the candles were extinguished the grimness sensibly increased, and he could feel all around him, thickly amalgamated with the ether, a superphysical presence, at once hostile and horrible. Then, to bring his terror to a climax, there issued from the bath a loud rubbing and splashing, as if someone, some very heavy person, was vigorously washing. The water rose and fell, squished and bubbled as it does when one is lying at full length in it, raising and lowering oneself, kicking and plunging first on one side and then on the other. Whilst, to add to the realism, Capt Smythe distinctly heard gasping and puffing; and the soft, greasy sound of a well-soaped flannel. He could indeed follow every movement of the occupant of the bath as graphically as if he had seen him – from the brisk scrubbing of body and legs to the finicky process of cleaning the ears and toes.'

If this was not unnerving enough, things rapidly got worse. Capt Smythe heard the door of a cupboard in the bathroom open and something sidled out and began to creep towards him. Paralysed with dread, Smythe found himself unable to move out of the path of the creeping thing. As soon as it touched him, he realised it was a woman, or the form of one: he could feel flounces of soft silk against his skin, heard the tinkle of jewellery and detected the scent of violets. Then the 'woman' stepped on him! 'Planting one icy-cold high-heeled shoe on his chest and the other on his cheek, she stepped on him as if he had been an orthodox cushion or footstool, purposely placed there for her convenience. A hollow exclamation, which died away in a gasp, issued from the bath, as the woman, with a swift movement of her arms, threw something over it. What followed, the Captain could only surmise, but from the muttered imprecations and splashes in the water, it seemed to him that nothing short of murder was taking place. After a while the noises in the bath grew feebler and feebler, and when they finally ceased, the woman, with a sigh of relief, shook the water from her arms, and, stepping off the Captain, moved towards the fireplace.'

Smythe's paralysis suddenly left him and he realised he wasn't in darkness at all, the candles were still lit. Floating in the air before him, rapidly fading, was 'a white luminous face ... entirely awful and devilish'. Smythe fled the bathroom – stark naked – and rushed downstairs to his entirely disbelieving and unsympathetic wife. A few days later, their eldest son ran out of the bathroom, horrified by the sight of something very nasty indeed in the bath: 'the body of a hoary-headed old man ... bloated and purplish blue'. Mrs Smythe and a servant hurried to the bathroom but found the bath empty and dry. As they left, however, they encountered on the landing outside 'a dark, handsome, evil-eyed woman' who silently glided into the bathroom and vanished.

Cured of her scepticism, Mrs Smythe ordered the household to decamp at once, and they never went back. Later they learnt that the house had previously been lived in by an elderly man and his much younger Spanish wife. The man had died in the bath but without a breath of suspicion falling on his young window, who accepted her inheritance and promptly left the country.

One of the more elaborate Victorian tombs in Glasgow's Necropolis.
Bill McKelvie/Shutterstock

MORE URBAN GHOSTS

A modern shopping mall seems an unlikely place for a haunting.
Nevertheless, the Wellgate Centre in **Dundee** became so
plagued by ghostly goings-on that the police were called in by
night cleaners concerned the place was being broken into. One
night a fire door opened inexplicably, setting off an alarm, and
cleaners heard voices and then footsteps walking over the roof.
The police found no one around. At the time it was suggested
one of the night staff may have unwittingly generated poltergeist
activity. It's also possible something spooky was disturbed when
old houses on the site were knocked down and the centre
constructed in their place.

Haunted shops exist elsewhere (for example, in Brunswick
Street, Glasgow, above). One of the stores in Cathcart Street,
Ayr, is haunted by a stately looking gentleman in a top hat and
a cloak. Some think he may be a senior manager dating from
the building's early use as a bank. Other ghostly phenomena
have also been reported, such as the mysterious moving about of
objects and voices heard from empty rooms. Another financial
centre, that of the financial office in Ayr's grand county council
buildings, is also haunted. The headless figure seen here may be
the apparition of a man who was executed on the site, for it was
once used as a prison.

In Union Street, the main shopping street in **Aberdeen,** a
weird presence known as 'The Clencher' has bothered a number
of people. The Clencher is an invisible but very physical spook
created by a brutal murder here in the early Victorian period. A
man named MacDonald was set upon by a gang of thugs. His
young daughter tried to restrain one of them by clinging to him

A headless ghost haunts the Ayrshire County Council offices.
Kristofer Keane/Shutterstock

for dear life. The lout became so infuriated at the girl's desperate attempt to save her father that he hacked at her with his knife, forcing her to let go. The wounds killed her. The Clencher is the echo of this tragedy: pedestrians in Union Street have suddenly felt themselves clutched round the waist by an invisible force. So tightly are they gripped that sometimes small pale hand-prints are left impressed on their skin.

Elsewhere in Aberdeen, a spectral cat haunts the Auchinyell area. Before it was built on, Auchinyell was a patch of marshy moorland called The Clash. The cat is said to be the ghost of one that leapt out of the darkness when a Mr Menzies was passing through The Clash at night, ripping out his throat and killing him. Presumably, this vicious beast was a Scottish Wild Cat, for no domestic breed of moggie would be capable of such a fatal attack.

Another strange story is told about **Perth**. When a Catholic priest, Charles McKay, arrived in the town to take over the missions there, he was approached by a local resident, Anne Simpson. She told him she had to speak to him urgently, that she had been waiting weeks to speak to a priest. The Rev McKay was greatly puzzled, for Mrs Simpson was a Presbyterian. He became even more confused when his visitor explained that a priest was not needed by her but by a ghost! Mrs Simpson told Rev McKay her nights were being disturbed by a troubled spirit which materialised in her room, demanding to see a Catholic priest. She recognised the apparition as a woman she barely knew named Maloy and was mystified as to why she of all people had been chosen for her unwelcome visitations. The ghost told Mrs Simpson that it could not rest until a sum of money which was owed at the time of her death was paid off.

The Rev McKay made some investigations and soon learnt that a woman named Maloy had indeed died recently. He then made a tour of the tradespeople in the town with whom she might have dealt and spoke to a grocer who was unaware of the woman's death and was able to confirm that she did owe him a small amount – three shillings and sixpence. The Rev McKay paid this trifling sum out of his own pocket. A few days later, Mrs Simpson came to tell him that for the past few nights the spirit of Mrs Maloy had failed to visit her. The priest told her about the small debt he had paid and a relieved Mrs Simpson went home free from ghostly persecution.

A ghost with a conscience formerly haunted Perth.
Stephen McCluskey/Shutterstock

In the 1700s poltergeist activity broke out in the minister's house in **Kinross**. Its behaviour was spiteful. It would rip and shred clothes hanging on washing lines and even while people were wearing them. On one occasion the entity threw the Bible on the fire. The book was rescued unharmed but when silver spoons were next thrown onto the coals, they melted with inexplicable speed. Every meal put in front of the minister, Mr McGill, had to be carefully checked because the spook would mix pins in with his food. Despite the careful scrutiny of Mrs McGill, a boiled egg was suddenly found to be stuck full of them like a pin-cushion – surely one of the most bizarre images in the long history of poltergeist manifestations.

In the same turbulent century, Bonnie Prince Charlie stayed at the venerable Thunderton House Inn in **Elgin** for several days before the fateful Battle of Culloden. When the pub was up for sale some years ago, odd things began to happen. For example, a standard lamp was seen to move all by itself across a living room. The lampshade was dislodged but otherwise it survived the spooky experience undamaged. Mysterious voices were heard in a corridor and, most evocative of all, the sound of ghostly bagpipes was heard emanating from a bedroom.

Prince Charles Edward Stuart also visited **Dumfries**, where he held court in a hostelry at the bottom of the High Street called the Blue Bell. For centuries after his visit the apparition of the bonny prince was said to be seen in the building (later renamed the County Hotel). In the Bloomsgate district of **Lanark** a spectral monk has been glimpsed in the cellar of the Clydesdale Hotel. The hotel is built on the site of a medieval monastery.

Two more haunted hostelries can be found in **Peebles**. The ghost of the Cross Keys Hotel in Northgate is former landlady Marion Ritchie, who died in 1822. She must have been quite a character in life, for she remains feisty in the afterlife. She can cause chaos – smashing glasses, moving objects around and switching electrical equipment on and off. When a former chef tried to take her photograph, he found himself pushed down a flight of stairs by an invisible force and he broke his leg. Another female phantom haunts the County Hotel in the High Street. She was a maid who, during remodeling work in the 19th century, came across a previously unknown tunnel leading from the dining room. She decided to explore it but became trapped. By the time she was found she had suffocated. This ghost too likes to move things about and occasionally makes her presence known with whispers and murmurs.

Among the more unusual haunted locations in Scotland was the Ravenscraig Steel Works in **Motherwell**, Lanarkshire, a town that used to be known as 'Steelopolis' before the industry went into decline. An indistinct figure dressed in boots and dungarees was frequently seen hovering about the No. 2 Blast Furnace. Sometimes he appeared to have no head. The identity of the phantom workman remained a mystery right up until the steel works' closure in 1992. Nothing now remains of Ravenscraig: the site has since been bulldozed flat.

The ghost haunting a factory in nearby **Wishaw** was firmly identified by former colleagues, even though it was never seen. The assumption was that the paranormal activity was down to Willie Primrose, a handyman who had died there not long before. Willie, who was known to hit the bottle rather too often, somehow managed to get himself locked inside one of the boiler rooms on a Friday night. His dead body was found on the following Monday. For a while afterwards the factory was plagued with mild poltergeist activity. The spook was particularly attracted to electrical equipment, turning various machines on and off and, most eerie of all, making the lifts go up and down by themselves.

The most famous of Scotland's industrial phantoms is surely the **Tay Bridge** ghost train. In 1878 the then longest bridge in the world was opened across the Firth of Tay, connecting Dundee with Wormit in Fife. At the time it seemed yet another wonder of Victorian engineering. Six locomotives were sent over it to prove its stability and Queen Victoria herself rode across the 2.75-mile span of iron and concrete. Tragically, the construction by noted engineer Sir Thomas Bouch was fatally flawed. He had assumed the River Tay had a bed of rock but when he found out this wasn't the case he tried to shore up his existing bridge with iron columns rather than coming up with a new design. Just a year after it opened, on December 28, 1879, disaster struck when a passenger train started to cross the bridge in a gale sweeping down the Tay estuary. The central span collapsed and the train, carrying seventy-five passengers, went down with it.

Ever since that fateful night, it has been claimed, a ghost train re-enacts its doomed journey across the Tay on the anniversary of the tragedy. Although the original bridge was never rebuilt – the current one stretches parallel to the foundations of Bouch's failed construction – a gloomy red light has been seen to follow its route at bridge height. The red light on the rear of the train was last thing seen by witnesses before it plunged into the river.

The magnificent Tay Rail Bridge runs parallel to the site of the original bridge which collapsed in a storm in 1879, just as a heavily-laden train was passing over it. Stephen Finn/Shutterstock

FIVE FAMOUS HAUNTS

Glamis Castle, in Tayside, is Scotland's most famously haunted house. Childhood home of HM The Queen Mother, Glamis has been the home of the Earls of Strathmore for more than six-hundred years. The abiding legend of Glamis is of a locked room and a secret too terrible to reveal. The 'secret' – not terribly well kept, in folklore at least – is supposed to be that a 'monster' was born to the wife of one of the Earls of Strathmore and kept hidden away in a chamber in the depths of the castle. The child grew into a huge, hulking creature possessed of enormous strength and it lived an impossible lifespan, perhaps for as long as two-hundred years. For all this time, the monster had to be fed and cared for in its secret room. The only people let in on the mystery were the successive Earls and a trusted servant or two. One source states that the 'monster' was born in the 18th century and expired as recently as 1921. Whatever the truth of the tale, there is no ghost story attached to it, so let's move on.

There are so many ghosts at Glamis there is no need to add a monster to the list. One of the most commonly reported is something of a monster, anyway: the wonderfully named Earl Beardie. He is described as being an enormous man in armour with a fierce expression on his hairy face. An inveterate gambler, Earl Beardie once loudly proclaimed that he would play the Devil himself if no one else was prepared to join him at dice. His Satanic Majesty duly obliged, with the inevitable result that the intemperate Earl gambled away his immortal soul. However, his ghost continues to gamble with something unseen and the rattle of his dice is said to still be heard after dark. His fearsome apparition has also been encountered stamping through the upper floors of the castle.

By contrast there is the peaceful presence of the Grey Lady, who quietly flits about Glamis bothering no one, despite her grisly history. She is believed to have been in life Janet, Lady Glamis, who was burnt at the stake as a witch in 1537 (and who is also said to haunt Edinburgh Castle). The woman haunting the garden has no choice but be quiet – she has had her tongue cut out! This distressing apparition is seen to run through the garden pointing frantically to her bleeding mouth. 'Jack the Runner' is another speedy phantom, seen racing through the grounds. The histories of these latter two ghosts remain obscure. Also unknown is the identity of the ghostly man with the tightly buttoned-up coat who walks through a closed door on a staircase. The little black boy who sits forlornly on a stone seat is thought to be the ghost of a Negro servant who was treated badly by his mistress.

Other ghostly phenomena associated with Glamis Castle include mysterious noises, 'shadowy figures' on a staircase and a door that wouldn't stay closed even when furniture was piled up against it. There is even a further story of a secret chamber. According to legend, in this room members of the Ogilvie family were hidden when they arrived at Glamis seeking sanctuary during a clan dispute. Choosing to side with the opposing clan, the then lord of Glamis sealed up the room and left the Ogilvies to starve to death. Ghastly noises were subsequently to be heard emanating from this room, which became known as 'The Haunted Chamber'. When the room was finally opened centuries later, the skeletons of the unfortunate Ogilvies were found within. So oppressive and eerie was the atmosphere which greeted the Earl who unsealed the door that he fainted. The Haunted Chamber can still be seen today, emptied of its gruesome occupants and brightly whitewashed but still possessing a distinctly creepy vibe.

Glamis is one of Scotland's most famous castles and also one of its most haunted.
Circumnavigation/Shutterstock

Allanbank in old Berwickshire (Borders) was another celebrated haunted house but one alas no longer standing. A former seat of the Stuarts, all that remains today of this historic estate are its barns, now converted into holiday cottages. Allanbank was haunted by 'Pearlin Jean'. Jean (or Jeanne) fell in love with Robert Stuart in Paris the 17th century. Tiring of his mistress and requiring a well-connected bride, Stuart left France and returned to Scotland. Jean missed him so badly that she scraped together enough money to travel to Scotland in the hope of rekindling their relationship. When she arrived, she learnt that Stuart was about to marry another woman. She hastened to Allanbank, just as her beloved and his fiancée were leaving the house in a smart carriage. Jean's hope evaporated in that moment and in her despair she threw herself under the horses. She was trampled to death.

From that time on Jean began to haunt Allanbank. She earned the name 'Pearlin Jean' after 'pearling', a style of lace she wore. The first sighting of the ghost was by a horrified Robert Stuart himself. She was sitting on the arch over the gateway where she was killed, her head bloody but unbowed. Then she took to patrolling the house, the swishing of her silk dress and her high-heeled footsteps echoing down the corridors as she opened and slammed shut doors. Unable to take any more sleepless nights, the Stuarts abandoned the house in the 1790s and leased it out. Unfortunately their departure did not stop Pearlin Jean making her nocturnal rambles and the Stuarts had to endure the complaints of a number of angry tenants. They sealed off the bedchamber she haunted most frequently but this only partially contained the problem. Ministers attempted to exorcise the unhappy ghost but with limited success. In the end the Stuarts sold off the contents and Allanbank was abandoned. It was knocked down in the early 19th century, thus ending the celebrated haunting of Pearlin Jean.

Spedlins Tower is a 16th century fortified house north of Lockerbie in Dumfries and Galloway. It was an ancestral home of the Clan Jardine but they abandoned it in the 19th century to live somewhere more modern and commodious. It began to fall into ruin almost at once but fortunately was privately purchased and restored to its former glory in the 1970s. It is now a private home.

A long-established ghost story is associated with Spedlins Tower: a rather horrible one. A miller, one Porteous, was accused of a misdemeanor, arrested and brought to the Tower. As the local baron, Sir Alexander Jardine had the right to try, imprison and, if he liked, hang criminals. Porteous was dumped in Spedlins' pit, a tiny windowless cell accessible only through a trapdoor in the ceiling. Shortly afterwards, Sir Alexander was unexpectedly called away to Edinburgh on urgent business. He left – completely forgetting about his prisoner.

After more than a week had passed, he suddenly remembered Porteous in the pit, starving to death in the bowels of his castle. He hurried home but it was too late: Porteous had died, slowly and horribly, from hunger and lack of air. For years afterwards the vengeful spirit of the miller haunted Spedlins Tower. A chaplain succeeded in binding the ghost in a hole in the ground, using a Bible which is still in the care of the Jardine family. Nonetheless local children claimed as late as last century that if you poked a stick through the keyhole of the empty Tower it would come back out with the bark chewed off by the still hungry ghost!

The semi-ruined Spedlins Tower photographed in the early 1900s.

'The Drummer of Cortachy is a well-known legend attached to **Cortachy Castle** and its owners the Ogilvys, Earls of Airlie. The legend is of a piece with many another weird story long current in Scotland, whose origin can only be vaguely guessed at, but whose existence shadows forth a very terrible picture of Scotland in medieval times.' So writes Charles Harper in his classic work on *Haunted Houses* published in 1907.

The story behind this traditional ghost does indeed reveal a taste for casual cruelty and habitual violence in those far off feudal days. There are in fact two versions of the legend to explain the

41

presence of The Drummer. The most commonly repeated is that he was a drummer boy belonging to a rival clan who was sent to Cortachy Castle to deliver a message of defiance to the chief of the Ogilvys. The phrase 'don't shoot the messenger' dates from the times when those delivering bad news risked bearing the brunt of the receivers' displeasure. Perhaps there was something cocky about the way the drummer delivered his message or perhaps the lord of Cortachy was simply a sadist, at any rate he became so angry that he ordered the boy to be sealed up in his own drum and then dropped off the battlements. The other version, stated by Dane Love in his *Scottish Ghosts* (Amberley), is that the drummer belonged to the Ogilvy clan but he foolishly risked having an affair with his lord's wife. When the illicit romance was exposed, the result was the same: he and his drum were thrown from the roof.

Unlike the phantom drummer of Edinburgh Castle, the Drummer of Cortachy is never seen. Only his drum is heard, beating out a mournful tattoo that is said to warn of a coming death, especially to members of the Ogilvy family. In this way he continues to deliver unwelcome messages. His most famous visit took place way back in 1844, when a Christmas gathering was being held at Cortachy Castle. One of the guests, a Miss Dalrymple, heard drumming outside her window late one night and, knowing nothing of the legend, blithely enquired of Lord Airlie at breakfast the following morning: 'Who is your drummer?' Her host went pale, as did his wife and several of the other guests. Miss Dalrymple had the sense to realise something was wrong and did not pursue her question. Later she was told of the ghostly omen and learnt that the last time the Drummer was heard, Lord Airlie's first wife died. When Miss

Dalrymple heard the drumming again that night, she made her excuses and left. The Countess Airlie died six months later, which confirmed in believers' mind that the Drummer's visit had been intended for her.

A few years later, in 1849, the Drummer was heard again, this time by a guest of the young heir to the estate while grouse-shooting on a moor belonging to Cortachy. He asked his Highlander guide where the drumming was coming from but the guide denied hearing anything, adding that such things were 'no canny'. Arriving at the shooting box as night was falling, he was informed his friend had had to suddenly go to London on hearing the news that his father, Lord Airlie, was lying dangerously ill. The Earl died that night. The Drummer has not now been heard for many years and hopefully won't again. Cortachy Castle, near Kirriemuir in Tayside, is still the home of the Ogilvy family. It is not open to the public but its gardens are and special events are regularly held in the grounds.

A sketch of Cortachy Castle by Charles Harper for his book on Haunted Houses, published in 1907.

If the legend of Cortachy Castle wasn't gruesome enough, we must now visit **Hermitage Castle**. Hermitage is situated near Newcastleton in old Roxburghshire (Borders) and is in the care of Historic Scotland. A great hulking edifice with vast, slab-like walls, this is no prettified country house and the legends attached to it are as grim and foreboding as its appearance. 'Bad Lord Soulis' is the most prominent figure in the history of Hermitage Castle and also its main ghost. William de Soulis was a 13ᵗʰ century contemporary of Robert the Bruce, a warlord with a reputation for bloodthirstiness and sorcery, an ugly combination. De Soulis was something of a Scottish Gilles de Rais, alleged to be both a black magician and a murderer of children. Legend has it he ate babies. He was not – to say the least of it – popular with his neighbours.

Bad Lord Soulis finally sealed his fate after a particularly brutal act of treachery. He invited a

An old illustration of the legend of the Drummer of Cortachy Castle.

nobleman, the Cout of Keilder, to a banquet but then, at a pre-arranged signal, had his men stab the Cout's retinue while they were tucking in. The Cout, who had remained on his guard and was a big man skilled with the sword, avoided the dagger intended for him and succeeded in fighting his way out of the castle. Unfortunately, in trying to cross Liddel Water, the river which runs past the castle, he drowned, held down by the spears of Soulis's men. On top of all the other murders and vicious acts laid at the door of Lord Soulis, this outrage prompted his neighbours to send a delegation to Robert the Bruce demanding his execution. If he would not stop at this level of treachery, he would stop at nothing, they argued – who would be next? The king agreed. Weary of hearing so many complaints against Bad Lord Soulis, he told the delegation: 'Hang him, boil him, do anything you like to him but for heaven's sake, let me hear no more about him.'

They took the king at his word. They succeeded in capturing Lord Soulis and then dragged him off to a nearby stone circle, where they wrapped him in lead and tipped him head-first into a cauldron of boiling water. He was very unpleasantly poached. Another victim of their rage was an enigmatic character known as Robin Redcap. Robin was a jester, companion or fellow sorcerer of the lord of Hermitage Castle. Some say he was his familiar spirit and not human at all. It is certainly a folkloric name, suggestive of fairylore. Bad Lord Soulis and the mysterious Robin Redcap now both haunt the castle.

Another horror story, similar to that attached to Spedlins Tower, appears to have more basis in fact. A 14th century owner of Hermitage Castle, Sir William Douglas, imprisoned a political prisoner, Alexander Ramsay in the dungeon. Here he was left to starve, his life bitterly prolonged for a number of days by grains of wheat which trickled down from a storehouse above his cell. Ramsay's groans of agony and despair are said to still be heard, echoing up from the place where he suffered his slow and painful death.

Of the other ghosts claimed to haunt this gaunt edifice, the most identifiable is the apparition of Mary, Queen of Scots. Her Majesty stayed at Hermitage Castle when James, Earl of Bothwell was in residence. She is described as 'a regal figure dressed in white'. More alarming are the, to quote Peter Underwood, 'terrifying ghosts in blood-stained armour glimpsed within the castle precincts both on dark and stormy nights and during the hours of daylight whenever there is lightning and the clash of thunder in the area'. It is unknown to which particular moment in the castle's violent history these grim figures belong. There are also reports of headless shapes being seen. When the influential paranormal investigator and journalist W T Stead visited Hermitage he was unnerved to hear what he described as 'the trampling of a multitude of iron-shod feet' clattering through the castle gateway, which then slammed shut, despite there being no human agent visible.

Spooky sightings still occur. In recent years a workman taking part in a restoration programme at the castle saw a face peering down at him from a window-space in an upper room – a room which had no floor!

Hermitage Castle has an even grimmer history than most Scottish castles, with ghosts that match its forbidding atmosphere.
Bill McKelvie/Shutterstock

MORE HAUNTED HOUSES AND CASTLES

One of the best attested examples of a haunting from the early years of paranormal research took place in Perthshire. Little now remains of **Ballechin House**, near Grandtully. It started life as a Georgian manor house built on the site of an earlier mansion belonging to the Steuart (or Stewart) family. By the time of the famous ghostly goings-on of the 1890s, the house only survived as one wing and was being rented out as a hunting lodge. Ballechin already had an uncanny reputation, however. The Major Steuart who had lived there between 1834 and 1876 had a keen interest in spiritualism and the occult. He believed in the transmigration of souls and in his final years made it known to all and sundry that he intended after his death to return in spirit form in the body of his favourite spaniel. It seems hard to credit but immediately after his decease, every one of his dogs – fourteen in total – were shot by his relatives, so as to prevent this unlikely scenario from occurring.

Twenty years later, tenants of the property were driven away by weird noises and other strange disturbances, prompting an enthusiastic member of the fledgling Psychical Research Society, the Marquis of Bute, to rent the place out for himself. He invited thirty-plus people to stay at Ballechin for what they believed would be an ordinary country house party. Most of his guests weren't interested in ghosts and knew nothing of the house's spooky reputation. Lord Bute hoped that should any paranormal activity occur, there was a good chance of it being experienced by a number of independent witnesses free of prior knowledge or expectation. He was not to be disappointed.

The range and frequency of inexplicable phenomena experienced during their residency at Ballechin is truly extraordinary. Charles Harper, in his 1907 book on *Haunted Houses*, sums them up rather well as a 'daily and nightly dish of detonating sounds in the corridors, the shuffling of slippered feet, the voices of an invisible man and woman in dispute, in which the words were indistinguishable [and] the sound as of someone reading aloud', to which was added alarming bangs against bedroom doors 'as if a very strong man was hitting the panels as hard as ever he could hit'.

There were also sightings of a number of apparitions. These included a hunchback-like figure observed by several people ascending a staircase; a nun who pottered about the house and garden; and a disembodied hand holding a crucifix which was seen by one guest at the foot of his bed. The most commonly seen ghost was that of a black spaniel, however, providing a strong link to the eccentric Major Steuart who had threatened to return as just such an animal. Guests also reported feeling an invisible dog pressing against their legs and hearing it 'snuffling' down the corridors. A series of séances appeared to connect to spirits called 'Ishbel' and 'Margharaed', Gaelic forms of the names Isabel and Margaret.

At the completion of this less than restful stay at Ballechin House, only one of the three-dozen guests was left unconvinced of the presence of ghosts. Most had experienced phenomena for themselves which they believed only the supernatural could explain and those few who hadn't agreed that constant vigilance, including nightly patrols, tended to discount trickery (and it would be a truly committed trickster who could continue the deception over the previous twenty-odd years). The events were written up by Lord Bute and another member of the Psychical Research Society in a book called *The Alleged Haunting of B——House* which attempted to outline and tabulate all the ghostly phenomena without bias (and without disclosing the location to avoid any future nuisance for the owners).

Charles Harper's 1907 sketch of Ballechin House which at one time was the most actively haunted house in Scotland.

Scotland boasts a wealth of haunted houses and castles, but there is only room for a handful to be included here. Some of these grand houses are so heavily fortified they might as well be considered castles and some of the castles have been so modified over the centuries by their aristocratic owners that they now look more like grand houses. **Traquair House**, near Innerleithen, Scottish Borders, is believed by some to be the oldest inhabited house in Scotland. It resembles a tough northern European version of a French Chateau. There are two ghosts at Traquair, although neither haunts the house itself. One is Bonnie Prince Charlie, who strolls up and down the avenue which was at one time the original entrance to the house. The other is a little old lady who potters peacefully about the grounds. Thanks to a portrait hanging in the house she has been firmly identified as Lady Louisa Stuart, wife of the last earl. Lady Louisa died in 1875, at the age of 100.

Another castellated manor house is **Abbotsford** in the County of Roxburgh. This is of much more recent date, however, having been built according to order by the novelist Sir Walter Scott in the 19th century. The man in charge of the construction was George Bullock, who also made some of the furniture in the house. At the moment when Bullock died, weird noises were heard throughout the house. Scott was so alarmed that he jumped out of bed, grabbed a claymore and went in search of intruders dressed in his nightshirt. It was only the next morning that he learnt Bullock had drawn his last breath at the same time. The ghost of George Bullock is one of the ghosts seen at Abbotsford. The other is Walter Scott himself. He is most often observed in the dining room, where his bed was set up during his last illness.

Abbotsford House, the former home of novelist Sir Walter Scott, is open to the public and boasts two ghosts, Scott himself and the builder of the house.
Jule_Berlin/Shutterstock

Balmoral Castle, in Deeside, is the Scottish home of the Royal Family and is as much a favourite retreat of Queen Elizabeth II as it was for Queen Victoria, who purchased it. It too is a 19th century mansion (Victoria found the original castle far too small for the needs of the royal household and had it replaced). The ghost dates from this time, for it is believed to be of John Brown, Queen Victoria's ghillie. John Brown became her close companion after the death of her beloved Prince Albert, his bluff commonsense and kindness helping her to overcome her depression brought on by grief. Their relationship was made famous by the 1997 film *Mrs Brown*, starring Judi Dench and Billy Connolly. John Brown's big, bearded form is most usually seen in the entrance hall, as if waiting for the Queen whom he served so loyally.

Inveraray Castle is the ancestral home of the Dukes of Argyll and shares with Traquair the resemblance to a French chateau, but much more elaborately so. It has often been described as a 'fairy-tale castle' thanks to its elegant proportions and its soaring turrets and towers. Here the traditional ghost is 'The Harper of Inveraray', whom, the old story states, was hanged by the frustrated Marquis of Montrose after he had failed to capture the Duke of Argyll during the religious conflicts of the 17th century. The current mansion was built after the old castle was torched by Montrose in 1644. The ghostly harper is rarely seen but on those few occasions he has been glimpsed, it's been noticed he wears the tartan of the Campbells, the clan to which the Dukes of Argyll belong. Usually, it is merely the sound of his harp that is heard. It is said his music can only be detected by members of the Campbell family, and then much more frequently by women rather than by men. Unusually for a ghost of this type, his rare visits don't appear to have any ominous meaning, such as warning of a death in the family (that honour is reserved for a phantom ship that sails over Loch Fyne to a place where St Columba formerly had a cell).

There is another ghostly sound associated with Inveraray, that of a commotion in the Green Library 'as though a whole shelf full of books had been taken out and thrown violently onto the floor'. No explanation has ever been forthcoming for this phenomenon. The other ghosts of the castle date, as do so many in this part of the world, from the Jacobite uprising. One is the sorry spirit of a young servant of the Duke of Argyll who was murdered by Jacobite soldiers. Having slain him, they chopped his body into quarters and stuck each part on the corner posts of the Duke's bed. This was intended as a warning to the Duke to drop his Hanoverian sympathies! A troop of phantom Redcoats has also been seen marching in the direction of Inveraray Castle.

The 'fairy-tale' Inveraray Castle replaced an earlier fortress but ghosts from those earlier days still intrude on the more modern building.
Bahadir Yeniceri/Shutterstock

A phantom piper is the musician haunting **Culzean Castle** in Ayrshire. Culzean started life as a Tower House, a modest fortification, but by the end of the 18th century it had been transformed into a splendid neoclassical mansion, where the Kennedy family lived in the grandest style. The piper has been seen and heard in the house itself but also in the grounds. A track through the woods is one of his favourite haunts and has been named 'Piper's Brae' in his honour. His piping is also said to be heard playing in a cave beneath the castle. The Culzean piper has a unique attribute. Tradition states that he plays his pipes before any member of the family gets married – a cheerful change from the usual omen of death.

Equally cheerful is the ghostly young woman who swishes through the house in a dazzling ballgown. Her identity is a mystery and it is unknown whether she has any other connection with the other ghost of Culzean Castle. This is rather distressing: the crackling of a fire can be heard and screams from somewhere in the depths of the house. An uncertain figure has sometimes been seen accompanying these phenomena, making its way through the house and standing on the oval staircase.

Gracious Culzean Castle has a phantom piper among its ghosts.
Grant Glendinning/Shutterstock

Unlike those considered above, **Brodick Castle** on the Isle of Arran is undeniably a 'proper' castle, a thickly stone-walled fortress dating back to the 14th century. It has two quietly haunting ghosts. One of these is a Grey Lady. She is thought to have been a maidservant who became pregnant by a Cromwellian soldier during the Civil War. Abandoned by him, she committed suicide. Another story to explain her presence is that she was a woman who contracted plague and who was locked away in a dungeon to keep her from infecting others and left to die. The other ghost is of a man wearing a long green jacket and breeches. He haunts the library. Also attached to Brodick is the tradition that the apparition of a White Deer manifests in the grounds to warn of the coming death of a member of the Hamilton family. Brodick Castle is now in the care of the National Trust for Scotland.

One of the most impressive of all Scotland's castles is the one that dominates the skyline of Sterling. A drab Grey Lady simply isn't grand enough for **Sterling Castle**: here the ghosts are of a Green Lady and a Pink Lady. They are both named after the colour of their gowns, of course. The tradition told to explain the Green Lady is that she was a lady-in-waiting of Mary, Queen of Scots and she saved Her Majesty from a horrible death when her bed-curtains caught fire. She has since remained behind at the castle to warn of any coming calamity (presumably to Stirling town rather than the currency, otherwise the poor thing would be appearing all the time!).

The Pink Lady was another brave lady, according to legend. She was the wife of a commander at Stirling Castle. When the castle became besieged by the forces of the English King Edward I in

1303, she refused to leave with the other women but stayed behind to help defend it, side by side with her husband. When the valiant defence ultimately failed, and Edward's army stormed the castle, her husband succeeded in convincing her to live to fight another day and she was sneaked out to safety. Her husband, however, was killed and now the sorrowing Pink Lady roams the castle in search of him.

Two phantom females haunt impressive Stirling Castle.
PHB.cz (Richard Semik)/Shutterstock

The ruined **Dunstaffnage Castle**, near Oban in Argyll, has an important place in Scottish history. It occupies the site of a stronghold which originally belonged to the Kings of Dalriada, the original Scots who came over from Ireland in the Dark Ages. Some claim it was to Dunstaffnage that they first brought 'The Stone of Destiny', which became incorporated into the throne used during the coronation of British monarchs at Westminster Abbey (the most recent, of course, being HM Elizabeth II). The Dunstaffnage Castle seen today dates from the 1200s and was built by the MacDougalls. It later came under the ownership of the Captains of Campbell. Flora MacDonald, the heroine who aided the flight of the defeated Bonnie Prince Charlie, stayed here in 1746.

Dunstaffnage is haunted by a Green Lady, an ancestral spirit as much fairy as ghost. She is known as 'Glastaig' or the 'Ell-Maid'. She is an ominous character, but the nature of the omen depends on her mood. If she is seen to be smiling, her appearance prophesies good fortune for the Campbells. If she appears to be sorrowing, the family will soon have reason to sorrow too. When she has nothing ominous to report, the ghost can be playful or annoying, tipping sleeping people out of bed being a favourite prank of hers. Most commonly she is heard rather than seen, her footsteps tripping along the passageways.

Finally we must consider **Balgonie Castle**, which is 'Scotland's most haunted castle', according to Richard Jones in his *Haunted Castles of Britain and Ireland* (2003). Balgonie, near Glenrothes in Fife, is very much a private home but the ancient chapel and courtyard is used for weddings. One of the best-preserved medieval tower houses in Scotland, Balgonie has played host to numerous celebrities over the years, including Mary, Queen of Scots, Rob Roy, Daniel Defoe and Samuel Johnson (together, as you might expect, with James Boswell). The castle was falling into disrepair as early as the middle of the 19th century, by which time it was already known to have a ghost. 'Green Jeanie' wanders the castle, her face hidden within a hood; just another of the anonymous ghostly women in green which are a staple of Scottish ghost-lore. Raymond Morris, the Laird of Balgonie, purchased the sadly decayed castle in 1985 and painstakingly restored it to its former glory and turned it into a comfortable family home.

The Morris family soon learned they would have to get used to sharing their new home with a number of unearthly lodgers. Margaret, the Lady of Balgonie, saw the apparition of a man in the dress of the 17th century peering at her as she dozed by the fire in an upper bedroom. She identified him as the 1st Earl of Leven, thanks to a portrait she happened to see some weeks later. Stuart Morris has seen several ghosts: a man and a dog, a head which emerged out of a wall in front of him, and an old man in the courtyard. The apparition of a soldier of the 16th century has also been seen in the courtyard. He stands in an awkward posture, with one arm outstretched. It was later discovered an outhouse had formerly been situated there and it is thought he may have been opening or closing its long-gone door.

The Great Hall, which has remained almost untouched since it was built seven-hundred years ago, is especially haunted. Here there has been seen a disembodied head, a white-clad spectre and various shadowy figures. A common manifestation is the sound of muffled voices heard in earnest conversation. Eeriest of all, a waitress once felt an icy finger creep its way down her back but there was no one to be seen when she spun round to find out who was being so familiar.

Historic Dunstaffnage Castle is haunted by an enigmatic ghost whose mood, should you meet her, might determine whether your future will be good or bad.
Bill McKelvie/Shutterstock

HOLY HAUNTED PLACES

Scotland boasts numerous religious buildings of great beauty and antiquity. Not a few of them are claimed to be haunted. We have already learnt of ghosts in St Giles' Cathedral and Greyfriars Kirkyard in Edinburgh. South of Edinburgh in Midlothian is one of Scotland's most celebrated churches: **Rosslyn Chapel**. Rosslyn has seen a considerable rise in its number of visitors thanks to Dan Brown's best-selling novel *The Da Vinci Code* (2003) which featured the chapel as the last resting place of the Holy Grail. Brown had been inspired to write his story after reading *The Holy Blood and the Holy Grail* by Michael Baigent, Richard Leigh and Henry Lincoln (1982), which aimed to trace Jesus Christ's bloodline down the ages, and a subsequent book which claimed that the Sinclair family, who commissioned the chapel in the 15th century, were themselves direct descendants of Jesus and Mary Magdalen.

Prior to all this pseudohistory, Rosslyn Chapel was justly famous for the extraordinary wealth of carving in its interior, the work of master masons imported from France. The architecture remains more than enough reason to visit this wonderful place. Elegant pillars and arches, striking roof bosses, charming angels, grotesque gargoyles and amusing scenes from rural life: hardly an inch of the stonework appears unadorned. One of the pillars is particularly outstanding. Known as the 'Apprentice Pillar', the carving it displays is exquisite, with a 'ribbon' of stone coiled round to connect an elaborate base and an equally fine capital. According to legend, William Sinclair presented the design for what became known as the Apprentice Pillar to the master mason, who, finding it beyond his skill, journeyed to Rome to examine the original. While he was away, a young apprentice decided to have a go at the pillar himself and succeeded where his master failed. On his return, the mason was so furious at finding he had been upstaged by his apprentice that he flew into a jealous rage and killed him. Rosslyn Chapel is now said to be haunted by the unlucky apprentice. One carving, showing a man, a boy and a weeping woman, are supposed to represent the mason, the apprentice and the apprentice's grieving mother. Some support for the truth of the story is that apparently special disposition had to be sought to get the chapel consecrated because a murder had been committed in it during its construction. The Chapel of St Matthew at Rosslyn (to give it its full title) is open to the public but is currently undergoing an extensive restoration programme.

An old engraving of Rosslyn Chapel, showing the Apprentice Pillar at left.

Far less well preserved than Rosslyn Chapel is the **Cathedral of St Andrew**, Fife. The Cathedral was built and rebuilt from the 12th to the 14th century. Situated close to the coast, bits of it kept being blown down in a succession of storms. It was abandoned after the Scottish Reformation of 1559 and stripped of its altar and other stonework. It is now a ruin but a number of towers still stand to a significant height. One of these is quite distinctive, rectangular in shape with two pointed turrets on either side. This is the Haunted Tower. The name is in recognition of the White Lady, a graceful ghost whose identity is a mystery. She strolls about the kirkyard near the tower, robed in white and wearing a veil and long white gloves. She was seen a great deal in the 19th century but occasionally still makes an appearance. In 1868 a room in the upper storey of the Haunted Tower was opened for the first time in many years and, among general lumber, there was found within it a pair of gloves just like those worn by the White Lady.

The tallest feature on the site is known as St Rule's Tower. St Rule or Regulus founded the original church on the site, which became a priory. St Rule is credited as bringing over to Scotland relics of St Andrew, in honour of whom the later cathedral was dedicated. St Rule's Tower belonged to the priory and therefore predates the cathedral, even though it is much better preserved. It can be entered and offers great views of the cathedral ruins and the sea. A phantom monk haunts St Rule's Tower. He is said to have been murdered here by a jealous rival nearly three-hundred years ago. The late paranormal investigator Andrew Green records an interesting encounter with the monk in his book *Our Haunted Kingdom*. A visitor was making his way up the tower's winding staircase when, in a particularly dark area, he found himself slipping on the worn steps. He clung to the handrail and gingerly continued his ascent. He said: 'I suddenly became aware of someone standing above me on the twisting staircase. He was wearing what looked like a cassock of some dark material with a girdle round his waist. "It's all right," he said in a low-pitched pleasant voice, "you can hang on to me if you like." "Thank you, but I can manage myself," I replied.'

The stranger moved to one side and the witness pushed past him to make the short ascent to the top. Something didn't seem quite right to him, however. The monk had been somehow insubstantial; on that narrow staircase he ought to have felt the physical presence of the man, even brushed against him, but it was as if there was nothing but empty space between him and the wall. Spooked, the witness hurried back down the stairs but failed to catch up with the mysterious monk. The custodian at the bottom said no one had exited the tower prior to the witness himself, nor had he seen anyone resembling a monk entering it. There is only one door into St Rule's Tower. The custodian informed him he had met The Monk of St Rule's.

*St Andrew's Cathedral, showing the distinctive 'Haunted Tower'
with its twin pointed turrets.*
Alessandro Colle/Shutterstock

Melrose Abbey in the Borders is a magnificent ruin, historically famous for being the burial place of Robert the Bruce's heart and architecturally for its beautiful rose-coloured stone and ornate carving, which includes a jovial bagpipe-playing pig. The Abbey Church of St Mary the Virgin started life as a Cistercian monastery in the 12th century but this was massively enlarged and developed from the following century onwards. The ghost of Melrose Abbey is Michael Scot, who was buried in the first abbey church in 1292. Scot was a noted scholar but as was so often the case in the medieval period, the studious were often mistaken for the fiendish because they dabbled in 'occult' matters like astronomy, astrology and alchemy. Scot entered folklore as a wizard and a necromancer skilled in the Dark Arts (we have met him before as part of the legend of Bad Lord Soulis at Hermitage Castle). Presumably this was not how he was perceived during his lifetime or his body would not have been buried on hallowed ground. A measure of just how sinister Scot's reputation became is that his ghost is said to appear not as a human being but as a serpent, slithering near his grave on the eastern side of the ruins (shades of Voldemort!).

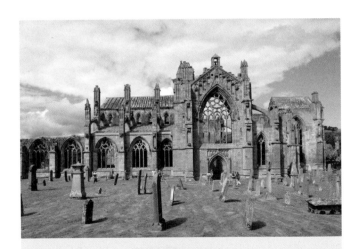

Melrose Abbey is the haunt of a medieval sorcerer by the name of Michael Scot.
MARTAFR/Shutterstock

According to the Historic Scotland website, it was at **Jedburgh Abbey** – another grand ecclesiastical ruin in the Borders – that a terrifying spectre prophesied doom to King Alexander III. In 1285 Alexander married his second queen, Yolande de Dreaux, in the abbey church and it was here, say Historic Scotland, that a spirit suddenly manifested among the congregation and warned the king that he would die in the coming year. The prophecy came true when, some months later, Alexander's horse panicked in a storm and threw him over a cliff. Other authorities place this event at the castle at Jedburgh during the wedding feast. In a scene which may have inspired Edgar Allan Poe's *The Masque of the Red Death*, a figure dressed in a shroud made its solemn way through the crowds of merrymakers, casting a pall, as it were, on the party. The furious king ordered his guards to grab the intruder, but to their horror and dismay they found the grave-clothes 'untenanted by any tangible form'. The grim figure, thus unmolested, continued its procession to the throne. It stood before the king, pointed to him, and vanished.

In his well-researched book on *Scottish Ghosts*, author Dane Love highlights a number of more modest churches with haunted reputations. St Mary's Church, **Haddington**, East Lothian, is haunted by the First Duke of Lauderdale, who is buried beneath one of the aisles. The kirkyard at **Kenovar** on the Isle of Tiree is haunted by the ghost of a sailor whose body washed ashore in the nearby bay. Black John Campbell, an unscrupulous tax collector working for the Dukes of Argyll, haunts the graveyard at **Soraby**, where he was cornered by a mob of angry tenants. Abraham Crichton, a merchant who committed sacrilege by demolishing an old church, later went bankrupt and was then thrown from his horse and killed – both misfortunes being seen by his neighbours as fair judgment upon him. After he was interred at **Sanqhuar**, Dumfries, his restless spirit took to haunting the kirkyard and the surrounding area. He was eventually exorcised by a minister who took with him a sword for protection.

Jedburgh Abbey is one possible setting for a legend of the time of King Alexander III. In recent years visitors have reported hearing the pealing of a ghostly bell among the ruins.

One of the most sacred sites in the whole of Scotland is the **Isle of Iona**, in the Inner Hebrides. Just off the coast of Mull, tiny Iona has been a holy place since Saint Columba founded a religious community here in the 6th century. Some sixty ancient

Scottish, Irish and Scandinavian kings have been buried here, testimony to Columba's reputation in the so-called Dark Ages and beyond. Today the medieval abbey which superseded Columba's monastery can be visited, along with the ruins of a medieval nunnery. There are also a number of splendid monumental High Crosses, more than a thousand years old. You might also like to visit the Well of Eternal Youth, blessed by St Brigit, but its properties are open to conjecture!

It would be a shame indeed if such a magical place could not offer some strange stories. The most commonly reported ghosts of Iona are, as you might expect, those of monks. There have been both Benedictine and Augustinian communities on Iona in addition to those of the earliest Columban period. The ghostly brothers have been seen sometimes singly and sometimes in small groups, not only inside the abbey but also in various places around the island. They are often accompanied by twinkling blue lights. Fairies have also been encountered on Iona. Other strange phenomena include an invisible force which prevented people ascending the old wooden staircase in the abbey buildings (since replaced) and three mysterious columns of smoke rising above an apparently deserted area of ground near Larachan Bay.

*The abbey church on the sacred isle of Iona, haunt of ghostly monks
and many other psychical phenomena.*
Michal Lazor/Shutterstock

Scottish author Alasdair Alpin MacGregor devoted an entire
chapter to 'Haunted Iona' in his *Ghost Book* of 1955. In it he
describes the experience of Johnnie MacMillan one moonlit
evening as he was making his way across the headland above the
beach known as White Sands. Suddenly Mr Macmillan realised
the croft he had been making his way towards had disappeared
and so too had a number of other familiar landmarks. He
stumbled down onto the beach 'in a state of mental confusion'
and then was amazed to see rounding an islet in the bay a host
of fourteen Viking long-boats.

'He could see the sweeping oars on each side of them as they turned in towards the north shore,' MacGregor relates. 'When they came a little nearer, he had no difficulty in seeing the old men and the young men they carried. It seemed as though they were shouting uproariously as if in exultation, though Johnnie MacMillan tells one that he himself could not hear a sound. Soon the galleys' occupants were leaping into the water, and dragging them towards the shore. Johnnie now turned aside to find, standing fifty yards or so away from him, a group of Columban monks, upon whom the invaders now flung themselves with murderous fury. He wanted to cry out in horror, but found himself to make any sound. When the invaders had disposed of the suppliant monks, they disappeared over the brow of the sandhills, in the direction of the Abbey.'

Mr MacMillan took note of certain emblems painted on the boats and experts at the British Museum later identified them as Danish and of the 10th century. The Vikings are known to have raided Iona in the year 986. Experiences in which people claim to have seen incidents from the past as if they themselves have been temporarily transported back in time to witness them are known as 'time slips'. Mr MacMillan's story has the hallmarks of a time slip, in that houses and other landmarks familiar to him had vanished from his sight even before he had his dramatic vision on the beach. However, he is not the only one to report such an experience. An artist, Bunty Cadell, painting near the Hermit's Cell on the island, abruptly found himself immersed in a battle between Vikings and islanders. The hectic and violent vision suddenly ceasing as quickly as it had begun, leaving Mr Cadell bemused and frightened.

One more time slip incident seems to have taken place when an elderly clergyman, who had been observed staring fixedly out to sea, walked out of the Bishop's House as if in a trance and then strolled calmly into the freezing waters of the bay. A friend who had followed him, shouted from the shore and, startled awake, the clergyman waded back to dry land. He said he had 'seen a vision of the abbey as it had been a thousand years ago' and felt compelled to take a walk along a causeway that had long since been surrendered to the ocean.

The White Sands on Iona, where phantom monks and Vikings have been seen.
Kevin George/Shutterstock

GHOSTS IN THE WILD

Despite its place in Scottish history, **Culloden Moor** in old Inverness-shire can still feel bleak and remote. A melancholy atmosphere seems permanently settled on the heath, making it feel lonesome and brooding despite the presence of a visitors' centre and any number of coach-loads of tourists or schoolchildren who may be roaming it at any one time. It was here, of course, that the Jacobite Rebellion rapidly came to an end. On April 16, 1746, Bonnie Prince Charlie's nine-thousand tired and hungry Highlanders met an equal number of government troops, most of them professional soldiers, under the command of King George II's youngest son, the Duke of Cumberland. In little more than an hour it was all over: the king's force had massacred the Scots.

It is said anyone of direct descent of any of the Highlanders killed at Culloden will be especially sensitive to psychic forces at the site should they visit on an anniversary of the battle. One story tells of a visitor from the United States, who riding across the moor on horseback in 1896, experienced an intense vision in which he found himself in the midst of the fighting. He saw and felt himself stabbed in the chest and he tumbled from his horse unconscious. When he awoke he was in hospital. He was told he had fallen out of his saddle and had sustained bruises. There was no stab wound, however.

Another incident involves a female visitor to Culloden Moor. She was exploring the area near the cairn-like memorial to the fallen soldiers when she noticed that a square of tartan, representing the Stewart clan, had fallen on to the grass. She began to pick it up but as she lifted a corner she saw lying beneath it the corpse of a young man in coarse-cut plaid also in the tartan of the Stewarts. Realising she was witnessing something uncanny, she replaced the cloth and hurried away. Other visitors say they have seen the bloody faces of soldiers reflected in the water of the Well of the Dead. A lone Highlander, shadowy and clearly not of this world, has also been seen at dusk near the memorial, bowed and pitifully weary.

The memorial cairn on Culloden. Several echoes of the fateful battle in 1746 have been seen in the vicinity of the monument.
Heartland/Shutterstock

In contrast to the Battle of Culloden, it was the Highlanders who were victorious in a clash in Perthshire on July 27, 1689. On that date three-thousand Scots saw off William III's troops on a hillside above the **Pass of Killiecrankie**, near Pitlochry. One the night before the battle, one of the Scots' commanders,

Viscount Dundee, woke to see a weird red light hovering by his bedside. The red light transformed itself into the figure of a man with its head matted with blood. The spirit indicated Dundee should rise and follow it and this, with some reluctance, he did. The spirit led Dundee to a window and pointed towards the plain of Killiecrankie. Then it disappeared. During the subsequent battle, Dundee hesitated over engaging with the English troops marching up the pass, reluctant to give up the advantage of the high ground. The memory of the appearance of the bloody spectre may well have spooked him. Finally, at sunset, he sent his force charging down the hill. It was perhaps as well he had delayed, for the timing turned out to be perfect. Within a matter of minutes, William III's army was defeated and its demoralised remnants were fleeing in terror down the pass.

But alas, the bloody-headed spirit of the previous night turned out to have been an ill omen after all. Dundee had no time to celebrate his victory: as he watched in triumph, a stray musket ball pierced his side and he fell, dead. Ever since, it is said, an eerie red light has been seen to glow over the Pass of Killiecrankie on the anniversary of the battle. It is thought to be the same light Dundee saw in his bedchamber but the bloody-headed spectre has not since been seen. Some claim to have witnessed a vision of the battle itself being replayed in the pass.

In the 1950s, two climbers camping in the wild and beautiful scenery of the Black Cuillins on the **Isle of Skye** were astonished to see a host of Highlanders haring across the bleak moorland before them. Their progress was entirely silent. On the following evening, the vision repeated itself but for some inexplicable reason, an hour later. This is only the best-known of a number of encounters with phantom soldiers around Skye.

The apparitions have become known as 'The Silent Ones' and sometimes number as many as fifty. On other occasions, only two or three Highlanders are seen at a time, making their noiseless way along Skye's narrow lanes or passes across the moors and mountains. Judging by their tartan, the ghosts belong to both the Macdonald and MacLeod clans, which formerly owned extensive parts of Skye.

Sandwood Bay at Cape Wrath is one of Scotland's finest beaches: a broad, golden arc of sand which is nonetheless usually deserted thanks to its isolation. The bay is also one of Britain's handful of haunted beaches. The ghost of Sandwood Bay is an aggressive one, indeed he acts as if the place belongs to him. The first recorded sighting was by a crofter and his son who had visited the bay to collect driftwood for the fire. Suddenly they realised they weren't alone on the formerly empty beach. Standing almost on top of them was a big man with a big beard, glowering at them furiously. They had neither seen nor heard his approach. He was apparently a sailor, wearing a cap and black reefer's jacket sporting tarnished brass buttons, and with worn heavy sea-boots on his feet. The sailor yelled at the crofter and his son, demanding that they leave 'his' beach at once and to give back that which 'did not belong to them'. They didn't argue, they dropped the driftwood and hurried away, recognising there was something decidedly uncanny about the bad-tempered stranger.

The spooky seaman was later seen by a ghillie, who watched him through a spyglass, concerned that he was poaching on the sand dunes. The ghillie went in pursuit but was disturbed to not only discover that the sailor had disappeared from view despite the open aspect all around him but also by the lack of footprints in the

Wild and remote Sandwood Bay is haunted by a ghost which has been known to warn people off the beach.
John A Cameron/Shutterstock

sand. Since these two early sightings, the ghost has been seen numerous times.

Far and away the strangest of the wild places of Scotland – stranger even than Loch Ness – is **Ben Macdhui**. Ben Macdhui is the highest mountain in the Cairngorms and the second highest in Scotland. It is popular with climbers, many of whom have reported peculiar experiences on its summit and the approaches. A booklet called *The Grey Man of Ben Macdhui and Other Abnormal Happenings*, published by the Edinburgh Psychic College in 1949, first brought the phenomena to the public's attention and much has been written about them since then.

The most commonly reported phenomenon is the sound of footsteps stomping along behind climbers and walkers on the otherwise empty mountain. A number of professional climbers as well as experienced amateurs, including a Professor of Organic Chemistry and a botanist from the University of Aberdeen, are among those who have heard the eerie footfalls. The cairn on the summit is one of the focal points of these sounds and it has been suggested they are made by the contracting and expansion of stones in the cold mountain air. However, the phenomenon seems too dramatic for such a simple explanation. Professor Norman Collie, an experienced mountaineer, reported his experience to the Cairngorm Club, as reported in the Edinburgh Psychic College booklet:

'Professor Collie was returning from the cairn in a mist when he began to think that he heard some other thing than merely the noise of his own footsteps in the snow. For every few steps he took, he heard a big crunch, as if someone was walking after him, but taking three or four times the stride of his own. Professor Collie said to himself, "This is all nonsense;" but he listened, and heard it again, though he could see nothing in the mist. As he walked on the eerie "crunch, crunch" sounded behind him, and he was seized with the most tremendous terror. Why, he said, he did not know, for he was accustomed to being alone upon the hills, but the uncanny something which he sensed caused fear to seize him by the throat. He took to his heels and ran, staggering blindly among the boulders, for four or five miles nearly down to Rothiemurchas Forest.'

This highly respected climber told his fellows: 'What you make of out of it, I do not know, but there is something very queer about the top of Ben Macdhui, and I will not go back there by myself, I know.'

The crunching of footsteps are not the only inexplicable noises to have troubled people on Ben Macdhui. Unearthly music has also been heard and also 'an enormously resonant Gaelic-speaking voice'. A few people have got a closer look at the Grey Man but their descriptions all vary, from 'a tall, stately human figure' to an apelike 'great brown creature' and a demonic entity 'with pointy ears, long legs and feet with talons'.

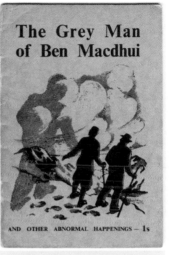

The Grey Man of Ben Macdhui

AND OTHER ABNORMAL HAPPENINGS — 1s

The mysterious goings-on reported from Scotland's second highest peak were first reported in this scarce booklet, a copy of which is in the author's collection.

The summit of Ben Macdhui is remote and inaccessible, only to be attempted by well-equipped and experienced mountaineers. It is unwise to attempt the summit alone, not only for the obvious reasons of mountain safety but also because the mysterious entity known as the Big Grey Man is still decidedly active, and he has been both seen and heard in recent years. The risk of encountering a gigantic phantom in the mist and then finding oneself running off a cliff in uncontrollable fright seems too much for even the most daring ghost-hunter!

The summit of Ben Macdhui in the Cairngorms, home of the terrifying phantom known as 'The Big Grey Man'.
Collpicto/Shutterstock